BARITONE T.C. (B♭ TENOR SAXOPHONE)

TRIOS FOR ALL

arranged by KENNETH HENDERSON and ALBERT STOUTAMIRE

CONTENTS

INSTRUMENTATION

V 1392 Flute (Piccolo)
V 1393 B♭ Clarinet (Bass Clarinet)
V 1394 B♭ Cornet
V 1395 E♭ Alto Saxophone (E♭ Baritone Saxophone)
 (E♭ Clarinet) (E♭ Alto Clarinet)
V 1396 F Horn

V1397 Trombone (Baritone B. C.)
 (Bassoon) (Tuba)
V1398 Baritone T. C. (B♭ Tenor Saxophone)
V1399 Violin
V1400 Viola
V1401 Cello & Bass

V1402 Piano-Conductor
 (Oboe-Mallet Instruments)
 (Harp-Guitar)

FOREWORD

A variety of combinations of instruments can play trios with these books. With the exception of the basses, any three like instruments such as three flutes, three clarinets, three cornets, three trombones, three bassoons, and so on can play together in three part harmony. Numerous dissimilar instruments such as violin, trumpet, and tuba also may perform all of the trios in these books. Basses must play the bottom line only, but the music is arranged so that they have the melody from time to time.

Any number of instrumentalists may play together in three part harmony. Thus, directors can rehearse the music with large ensembles and assign trios of players or groups of players to practice and perform together.

This set of books meets the needs of friends and neighbors who wish to play together for festivals, concerts, or just for fun, whether or not their instruments are traditional combinations. The pieces also make excellent material for auditions and sight-reading.

FEATURES

The material covers a wide range of styles and music by composers from Baroque through contemporary eras.

The trios range in difficulty from grades I through IV.

The pages are laid out in an identical manner in each book so that performers can quickly locate a point for discussion or rehearsal. No page turning is required when playing.

SUGGESTIONS

When high sounding instruments and a low sounding instrument (violin, trumpet, and tuba for example) play a trio, the high instruments play the upper lines while the low instrument plays the bottom line. Bass clarinets, tuba and contrabass instruments always play the bottom line only.

Interesting effects can be obtained by combining several trios of instruments. Three violins may play trios simultaneously with three cellos. Three flutes, three clarinets, and three bassoons make an interesting triple trio group. Three cornets and three trombones blend well as a double trio. Also, several like instruments (horns for example) can play the top part in unison while several other like instruments (trombones for example) play the second part and basses play their part (the third line).

RIGADOON

HENRY PURCELL

IVAN SINGS

ARAM KHACHATURIAN

ANDANTE

W. A. MOZART

THEME
(from Symphony No. 1)

JOHANNES BRAHMS

HUNTER'S SONG

L. VAN BEETHOVEN

PASSEPIED

GEORG PHILLIP TELLEMANN

MENUET

Allegro grazioso

G. F. HANDEL

ANDANTE GRAZIOSO

FRANZ JOSEF HAYDN

LITTLE MARCH

DMITRI SHOSTAKOVICH

SOLDIERS MARCH

Tempo di marcia

ROBERT SCHUMANN

BALLET ANGLOIS

JOHANN K. F. FISCHER

DIRGE

BÉLA BARTÓK

MARCH

S. PROKOFIEV

WALTZ

EDVARD GRIEG

DANCE

DMITRI KABALEVSKY

KAMARINSKAIA

P. I. TSCHAIKOWSKY

LARGHETTO

IGOR STRAVINSKY